SILENCE NO MORE

MY STORY ~ MY LIFE ~ MY DELIVERANCE

WOMAN TO WOMAN CONFERENCES

All scripture quotations are taken from *The King James Version* of the Bible. (KJV) Public Domain.

Cover and interior illustrations by Eboni A. Sampson

Associate Editor: Parrish A, Sampson

Sampsonite Publications

Woman To Woman Conferences
A division of Kingdom Word Ministries
San Diego, California
www. Ccl-kingdomword.org

ISBN-13: **978-0692310854**
ISBN-10: **0692310851**

Printed in the United States of America

Awesome!

"When women in the Body of Christ become transparent in sharing with others how God delivered them from the "Raw to the Real" they have only one purpose in mind, to let you know that you are not alone in your pain, hidden sin or confusion.

Apostle Lunette Sampson writes with an open heart of compassion and exposes the tricks and lies of the enemy that drag some into perversion, promiscuity and plain old sin.

The Woman of God is the heartbeat of God that keeps true friendship together and families from parting ways.

I am so very proud to have read her book "Silence No More" and pray each person that reads it becomes a springboard of truth that brings deliverance to others.

Although it is her story others, have been silent too long and it is time to get free.
Thanks Apostle Lunette Sampson for becoming the declaration that others will cling to."

Apostle Robin Blue
Robin Blue Ministries

Revolutionizing!

"Silence No More is a revolutionizing book that will set you free from not only sexual abuse but abuse any of kind, past hurts, pains and additions. This book will set you on path of freedom that will help you walk and live out your God given destiny. You will not be able to put this book down until you finish reading it from cover to cover. Thank God for Apostle Sampson revealing her past to set people free. We pray that every person that reads this book and has unresolved issues in their lives will be changed by the power of God."

DRS. Wilton and Yolanda Holmes
Victory in the Truth Ministries
Mesa, Arizona

This book is dedicated to my three daughters Marrena, Eboni and Parrish. Thank you for loving me and standing with me through it all. To my precious granddaughters Zyonna and Mishael, and to my" ride or die" goddaughter Quawana who stands by my side with love and support. Also to my many spiritual daughters, and the many women who suffer in silence, may you find your voice through this book.

ACKNOWLEDGEMENTS

I give thanks to my Lord and Savior Jesus Christ for His grace and mercy toward me in all of my fumbles; to my precious children for allowing me to be so candid about our family life, and to my dear friends Apostle Ramona Haswell and Tracie Wooden Carlisle for their help and guidance.

CONTENTS

FOREWORD

Apostle Lunette Sampson offers years of personal experience, knowledge, and ultimately wisdom in how to walk in freedom after years of low self-esteem and unworthiness. She holds nothing back as she tells riveting stories of her pain. She takes her readers on a journey into her openly painful childhood exposing the depths of shame, degradation, and humiliation as she tried to find her identity. Her transparency is relevant for women today who have in the past, or are currently experiencing sexual and emotional trauma, and have made wrong turns and decisions because of memories of betrayal, rejection and abandonment.

Time and time again she relives her pain through her written words as she bares her soul, exposing herself in a way that most would not have the courage to do. Her purpose here is to demonstrate that although many have undergone countless years of pain, there is hope and help for those who diligently seek after it. Lunette guides you into a transformative reality with many examples of how God touched her life during her healing process. *Silence No More* reveals that no matter how bad you think your life is or may have been, you can be set free from mind-bondage. You can overcome thoughts that have kept you enslaved in your mind causing you to believe you are not good enough and will never overcome. Emotional and mental healing is sure to come while the pages of this very important work reach out and grasp your heart.

Whether you've lived a life of confusion and chaos, or masqueraded as someone who has it altogether, I guarantee you'll find yourself somewhere in this book. Lunette emerges from being a powerless victim living a dysfunctional existence, to a powerful woman of God leading many other women into their God ordained destinies. She reminds the audience that liberty and freedom are attainable.

Dr. Gayle Rogers, Ph.D.

Forever Free INC. &
Coaching for Empowerment

INTRODUCTION

Never once in my life did I ever think I would tell this story, because in reality the shame was too great for me to bear. For many years I not only carried the secret of my molestation, but I lived under a certain bondage that secret created. Back in the days when I was growing up no one ever talked about sexual molestation around me. I never even heard anything after I had become an adult so I had no idea how serious the matter was. Sometimes society chooses to think the 1950's were the innocent years, but evil men existed then just as they do today. The only difference today is that people have learned to be more protective of their children. We are now more aware of what can happen when our eyes are closed.

Few people understand the depth of damage a person who has been sexually assaulted incurs. Without help from God, the damage can be virtually irreversible. Sometimes

13

we can find ourselves so needy we act out as though we are sexually insatiable. Being driven by this we look for love in all the wrong places. We don't know those are spirits that have been transferred to us through inappropriate touch. We feel this is just the way we are. We accept this about ourselves without understanding something has occurred that created those feelings. Lost and lonely, we often make unhealthy choices that can literally keep us off course for the rest of our lives.

In this book I bare myself in hopes that your eyes will be opened enough to confront your issues. Some mountains will not move from your life unless they are confronted head on. I know how much courage it takes to do this, but God is right there with you to give you the strength you need. If we don't make the effort, nothing will change for us.

When God set me free I got a new lease on life. For the first time in 49 years I was truly free from the secrets and the cover up that made me so ashamed. However, I thought I was the only woman going through this. God has since revealed there are literally millions of women who suffer in silence for one reason or another. My prayer today is for your complete healing as these truths are unfolded to you. May your life be forever changed in Jesus name.

My Story
The Beginning

Chapter One
Unguarded

I can't remember how old I was when I had my first sexual encounter. What I do remember is I was so young the bathroom sink looked tall to me; so my guess would be I was about two or three years old. I was so young in fact I didn't know what was really going on. These molestations continued in my life by the same man for many more years to come. As I can remember it, the first time I realized anything was wrong with what this man was forcing me to do to him, I was probably about six years old. I am sure he must have told me something that caused me to keep my silence even though that part escapes me right now.

Still I believe even at six years of age I was smart enough to realize that if I told my Grandma it would have caused a big family confusion. You see this man was not only a close family friend; he was also my cousin's father. The mere thought of what would come out of this frightened me to death.

Until God opened this up to me I never knew how many women had similar experiences. We have kept our silence for various reasons, and some of you really may feel those experiences are so far in the past there is no need to bring them up now. I thought so too. I thought I had been one of the lucky ones and my life was unaffected by it, but I was wrong. You are wrong too if you think it just all went away. Perhaps you have buried the painful memory deep in the back of your mind. You may have buried it so deep you don't remember much about it at all. I will show you in my story the effects of that experience are probably still there. Even if you are a born again

Christian believer you may still be experiencing the residual from your sexual assault.

Through my childhood years I continued to be molested by this man. It appeared to be some kind of penalty or fate that life had imposed upon me for reasons that were extremely unclear to me. When I look back now I realize that my young life was littered with questions, and there was no one there to provide answers. I was always so alone and this secret threw me into an even deeper depth of loneliness. After all who could I share this with?

As the story goes, John was a Merchant Marine. He worked on merchant ships and he was gone a lot of the time, but when he would return you could be sure he would find me. I don't even know how he knew what school I went to or anything, but often he would show up at my school to lure me with gifts and trinkets. It made me feel kind of special to have someone care enough to bring me gifts. My Grandma was raising me and she was crippled, so she couldn't come to school to see about me. This made me easy prey for his attentiveness in this area. I later learned that caring had nothing to do with it. He just knew my family situation and took advantage of me because of it.

You see both of my parents were heroin addicts. My father fought in the Korean War and he came home already drug addicted. My mother on the other hand became addicted following my father, I suppose. I don't know, but however it happened I was severely neglected so I was given to my paternal grandmother. Thank God she was willing to take me or the authorities would have put me in an orphanage. That was the only alternative in those days. I will always love her for how she took care of me although one of her weaknesses was alcohol. She would drink and get drunk, and then she would fall asleep sitting up in the chair. That is how John got access to me. He knew if he came by with a bottle of booze he could get her drunk, and when she would fall asleep he could do what he wanted with me.

Before I entered the fourth grade my father died from a drug overdose. He had just been released from prison after serving three years. Three years in the life of an eight year old is a very long time. I missed him so much. Just having him around made me feel so loved and secure. My Daddy was a tall handsome man with a head full of curly black hair. All the women chased after him. He was talented too. He played the French horn and when he was home you could always hear the riffs from his horn as he practiced his jazz. He was so intelligent. He knew all sorts of things, and I used to love to ask him questions about everything. He would always try to provide answers for me. I don't believe he ever said "I don't know". He spoke French fluently too, and he even taught me a few words. I was sure my Daddy loved me. No one could tell me anything else. Maybe my mother didn't care about me, but I was sure

about this one thing; my Daddy loved me! I
knew this because my grandmother always told
me so and I believed her.

I remember it like it was yesterday.
Daddy made his thirtieth birthday on April 3rd
and before a week had passed he was dead. I
will never forget the shock and the pain I
experienced from his death. I had hopes and
dreams one day we could be a real family, but
alas, all hopes were gone along with my father's
life. It was so sad. He had shot up after being
clean for so many years and it killed him. I felt
as though I was literally drowning in a sea of
loneliness all over again. My mother who was
never around anyway, was probably
incarcerated at the time herself. I seem to
remember her coming to the funeral parlor for a
special viewing of his body with two armed
guards. They brought me there so I could see
her since I hadn't seen her in such a long time.
Seeing her did nothing for me at all. She was
always like some stranger to me. I knew she

was my mother only because they told me so. The times when she would come around she would try to fill my head with ideas of grandeur about what she was going to do for me and how wonderful it would be, and then I wouldn't see her for a really long time again. It was all just talk and I learned that early in the game, so to protect myself from disappointments I hardly listened and tried never to believe her.

Getting back to my story let me mention something here. John (my molester) was not having sexual intercourse with me yet, but he was still fondling me and encouraging my favors upon him. Then at age twelve or thirteen he introduced me to pornography. This is where I learned about real perversion, and as a teenager this mess occupied a great deal of my thought life. The sixties was the time when sex was really opening up publicly, and it was becoming easier and easier to get hold of the smut. I had an aunt and cousin who lived with us and the both of them would read sexually explicit books all of the time. After they finished with them they gave them to me to read. Can you honestly believe they would give a young teenager such stuff? When I would get a hold of these books my imagination would soar.

In those days the censors did not allow any kind of vulgarity on television. Everything you viewed was pristine and perfect, but in the real world filthy men and women were everywhere. Being alone put me in position to encounter filthy pedophiliac men all of the time. They would approach me in the movies, in the park and even at family gatherings. I can't tell you how many times my uncles have said inappropriate things to me. One of my uncles even touched me under the pretense of teaching me how to ride a bike. As if that wasn't enough, I was fondled by an x-ray technician once at the hospital. So much of this went on in my life I was sure something was wrong with me. It never made me feel pretty or wanted. It just made me feel dirty and lonely. In the house where we lived my cousin had men coming over for booty calls all of the time, and my aunt and her man were always doing something nasty with the door open. I was surrounded by freaky people without ever realizing how abnormal it was. How could I have known? I had seen these things going on around me almost all of my life. It was not surprising I lost my virginity to a young teenaged boy at the age of fourteen. I was feeling desperate to have someone like me, so I used my sexual knowledge in hopes of getting him to care about me. Of course it didn't work. All it really got me was a three minute lay.

Just around that time I met my first husband. There was a group of us kids who used to hang out together. We had a clubhouse in the basement of our apartment building and someone in the group invited him to our clubhouse. He wasn't much to look at, but he appeared to be a nice guy. Why he would want to be with our bunch escaped me since he was at least five years older than most of us. Never the less, we found each other's company and we seemed to enjoy being together. One day my girlfriends and I played hooky from school and I ended up getting sloppy drunk. No one was willing to take me home in that condition so they called him to come for me. He took me to his house and put me in his bed just to sleep it off. When I woke up it was night and I was scared out of my mind to go home. It kept getting later and later, and I became more and more afraid, so I spent the night with him. That was the first time I ever stayed out all night, but after we hooked up it was only one of many. I can only imagine the worry I put my Grandma through. Before long she and my family found out I was involved with this young man. They made a big deal out of it because I was only fourteen years old while he was nineteen. My family thought he was using me for sex, but he wasn't. He was afraid to do something like that because I was still a minor. I was so naïve that I didn't even know he could go to jail for having sex with me. As I remember it though, he held out as long as he could, but before too long I seduced him. I really wanted him to love me so I gave it my all. By golly it worked! We fell head over heels in a lust that really felt like love. It made me feel good to know I had that kind of power over a man. Two years later we were married. I was sixteen years old by then. My mother (who magically emerged from her preoccupied life a few years earlier) was afraid I would shame the whole family with an unwanted pregnancy, so she signed for me to get married. At sixteen I was such an emotional mess even the wedding was sort of a blur to me. We got married in my mother's living room. Without any involvement from me she set everything up. Family and friends alike were there with smiling faces. I'll bet under those smiles they were secretly wondering what was really going on? No one dared to say anything though. My maternal side of the family had always been very skilled at cover ups so they just kept on smiling. Fortunately none of it registered with me anyway. I was so emotionally out of sorts I barely remember who married us, who the bridesmaid was, best man, or anything else. Looking back now I am sure I needed professional help, but in those days African American people didn't have that sort of thing available to them. All I can tell you is this. After I got married instead of the "happily ever after" thing I always read about in books, things got increasingly worse for me.

Chapter Two
Happily Never After

My husband was a Pastor's son and he was raised in the church. Since he was only nineteen when we met he probably just had a bare minimum experience with women. To me he was an older man who knew so much more than I did. He appeared to be so mature, but as I see it now he was just a baby. I knew he wasn't a virgin because he told me stories about some older women he had relations with. Still with my insatiable sex drive I am sure I was a lot for him to handle.

About a year after we met he went into the Navy so he was either away on the ship, or stationed at the Brooklyn Navy Yard. As I mentioned before, things were far from right with us. All he wanted to do was hangout with his friends. He often stayed out all night too. Remember now I was still very young so the only staying out all night I had ever done was with him. What did men do when they stayed out all night I wondered? Why was he always leaving me home alone? Didn't he know that made me feel like a rejected little child? The whole time he was out there I stayed awake looking out of the window for his return. Finally he would come home as though nothing ever happened. I would be so happy. The first thing I would do is jump on him kissing and enticing him. Being in the bed is all I ever wanted to do because it was the only thing that made me feel loved and secure. I thought if I could give him enough sex it would make everything okay and he would want to be with me more. NOT! Hindsight tends to be 20/20 so I can now see how that worked against me instead of in my favor.

In my loneliness my sexual thoughts ran crazy and my neediness increased to the point where I was simply overwhelmed. The only time I had any peace was when I was in bed having sex. He would hug me and hold me then. Those hugs expressed his love for me. Yet I was more of an emotional mess than ever. I couldn't get enough. I really didn't know what to do with myself. I was unhappy and miserable inside most of the time. This caused me to begin making shameful choices and decisions. I found myself sleeping with other men I just met on a humbug. I knew cheating was not the answer, but desperate and driven I did it anyway. I needed someone to give me the attention I so desperately craved.

Internal chaos was the order of the day for me. Then as if that wasn't already enough, my husband started to physically abuse me. I am not the kind of woman who will just stand there and let anyone beat on me. I have always been a fighter, so we fought like animals lick for lick.

Sometimes we would literally break the lamps, tables and chairs. Occasionally someone would call the police on us. It was that bad! Why I stayed in that misery I am not sure of till this day? I guess some of it had to do with me not knowing where to go. I had always been so alone in the world anyway and I never had anyone to protect me, so I remember thinking to myself, who would even care enough to help me? My mother was around, but heck she never did anything but cause me misery. Grandma was there and I knew I could probably go back home, but home hadn't been much of a happy place either. So I stayed and suffered in silence with no one to tell.

Before his time was up he had gone AWOL and it resulted in him being dishonorably discharged from the Navy. In spite of that he somehow still managed to get a decent job. He worked at the nearby public school as a Teacher's aide. He made a fair salary I suppose, but I never got any of it. His claim was his mother made him give her his paycheck. She owned the building where we lived and she and my father in-law occupied the apartment downstairs from us. I never knew what went on with that family. They were always so strange to me, so I got a job and made my own money. I worked as a switchboard operator for an answering service and that kept me busy most of the time. It helped the misery some, but we still didn't get along well. We continued to fight and fight.

One day I heard the family talking about a brother from California who was coming to New York to run a revival at my father-in-law's church. Everyone was so excited and great preparation was being made to accommodate him and his crew. Before long the big day finally arrived. I was pleasantly surprised at how loving and kind these people were. My mother-in-law had been quite the opposite toward me. She was so strict and mean. I was told she was that way because she was saved.

When my brother in-law arrived he had an Evangelist with him who made a point of reaching out to me. She must have discerned how deeply distressed I was. She kept telling me Jesus loved me and He wanted me to give my life to him. Since I was not raised in a Pentecostal church I wasn't sure about this saved thing they talked about so much. It all seemed a little scary to me, but I enjoyed the attention and love she gave me anyway. I needed it so desperately. On that Tuesday night the Revival started. Everyone in the family was going to church, so I went too. I put on my best outfit which was a little white low cut dress I had made myself. It was all I had. Thank God no one made me feel uncomfortable about it or I may not have gone with them. I guess the singing and preaching was pretty good that night although to this day I couldn't tell you what the message was about. What I remember the most is when the Preacher made a call for prayer I went up. I knew my life was a mess and I figured some prayer might help me a little. I didn't know he was making an altar call, I just wanted prayer. I had been to their churches before and seen the great display of dancing and falling out they did, but I didn't want any of that because it frightened me. I believed that people could get happy enough to dance, however the falling out thing looked pretty phony to me. In my heart I wanted Jesus to help me although I wasn't even considering giving my life to Him. When the man of God prayed for me the power of God overtook me and laid me out as though I was in a cloud. I had never felt anything so wonderful in all my life. By the time I came to myself people were over me praying and screaming "Thank You Jesus"! All I wanted at that point was to get up from there. That's where my focus was at the time, but upon collecting myself I realized I felt very different. I didn't consider it was called something because I wasn't familiar with that stuff. All I knew was I no longer wanted to do anything that would not please God anymore. In an instant God had changed my life. I seemed to have peace for perhaps the first time in all of my life. I was so peaceful inside that I could barely speak above a whisper. Oh yes, without a doubt I was changed, because on the following Sunday I was ready for church bright and early. No one had to ask me anything. This time I couldn't wait to get there. I could hardly wait to experience that wonderful feeling again, so when the Pastor made a call for prayer, I eagerly jumped right up and went to the altar. At first nothing happened and I thought it wouldn't come, but then suddenly there it was! It washed over me and laid me out like I was in a cloud again. This time the Holy Spirit took over my tongue and I began to speak in another language. I was so happy. Tears were just flowing down my cheeks, tears of pure joy. I was so happy inside I honestly had to laugh to myself. Wow! Everyone was so happy for me at church too. They seemed to be completely ecstatic over my new experience. In my excitement I couldn't wait to tell my husband.

Oh by the way, he was the only one in the family that didn't come to church for this event therefore he wasn't around to see all the good stuff that was happening to me. Today I would *have* to tell him about this one because this was just too wonderful to keep to myself. Do I need to tell you what his response was? He seemed even more disappointed in me than before. What a slap in the face! I thought surely he would love me now, but he acted as though he hated me more since Jesus was in my life. His reaction was so baffling to me.

Well at least some things had changed in me. I could feel the presence of God with me all of the time. As usual my husband did his own thing, but being alone was not the same for me anymore. Now I had peace of mind. I also had an internal joy that bubbled inside of me all of the time. There was also something else that I really enjoyed, going to church. Church was a wonderful place. I felt loved and welcomed there, so I spent as much time there as I possibly could. Yes the change in me was evident, except for one thing. I had always had a crazy love for my husband. I loved that man so much sometimes I could hardly stand it. There of course was almost no reciprocation. The closer I tried to get to him the further away he went from me. Occasionally I could still lure him into bed with my little bag of perverted tricks. Oh yeah, I was still quite freaky, but I could never capture his heart. In the back of my mind I thought the marriage should count for something at least he's still mine.

In the days that followed the abuse and rejection continued. There were times when he would come in angry and just take it out on me. One time he came in and called me into the kitchen. Out of nowhere he just slapped me with all his might. I tell you he slapped me so hard I saw stars for real! He never told me what it was for. On impulse I ran into the bathroom and locked the door. Although I was no wimp when it came to defending myself, that time he hit me so hard it frightened me. When I came out he was laying on the bed as though nothing happened. After I got myself together I was ready to go at it, but he never said anything to me. Every now and then his older brother would try to talk some sense into his head. You know the old "you have a good wife" talk? Well he wasn't having it. That old talk did nothing to change our relationship. Our situation even began to worsen because now he was drinking all the time. It appeared to me that overnight he just decided to become a drunk. Now you *really* couldn't depend on him for anything. When holidays would come around I would fix the house up and try to make things nice for our little family. He either wouldn't show up, or when he did he was plastered and would pass out.

Six months had passed now and I was still holding on to Jesus. One day one of the in-laws told me their brother who previously preached the revival was coming back. Apparently he was coming to take any of the family back to California with him that wanted to go there to live. I got excited right away. I thought maybe a change of environment was what we needed to help our marriage. I remembered how loving and kind they had all been to me and a glimmer of hope came into my heart. I talked it over with my Honey and he agreed a change of environment would probably be a good thing. However, he decided I should leave with his brother and he would follow in about six weeks when his mother and father would be making the trip. I agreed to do it without ever thinking there was any reason not to trust him. Do I need to tell you six months passed and still he never arrived? His parents were having some complications with selling the house its true, but he only called me once in all that time. I didn't have the freedom to use a phone whenever I wanted to so I couldn't call much, but when I did get a chance to call he was never home. Then after a while the phone was disconnected. I sent letter after letter but still I got no reply.

Those six months I spent without him had to be the worse six months of my entire life. I was lonelier than ever since he never called or wrote. I suppose I was in denial or something about the reasons for my not hearing from him. Everyone was still sweet and kind to me, but that didn't do much to help my situation. I was still lonely and unhappy, and you know what happens to me in those lonely times. My mind would begin to run crazy with sexual thoughts. No, that stuff had never really left me. I had not cheated on my marriage since I was saved, but all the perverted thoughts and fantasies were still there. The only reason I was not consumed by them was my involvement in Church. The Church kept me occupied and in touch with my spiritual side. However, in the face of extreme circumstances these thoughts became full blown, and even church activities couldn't keep the night time misery away. I could sense I was becoming spiritually weaker. The weaker I got, the more the thoughts flooded in. It was madness. All kinds of sexual images flooded my mind on a daily basis. To make matters worse, we lived in the country and it was springtime. Everything was mating right out there in the open; pigs, cows, dogs and oh yes, the rabbits. Once I even walked up on my brother in-law and his wife by accident. Everyone and everything was engaging in sex except me. I felt so abandoned. I had no one to make love to me, so I made love to myself. That was a nasty little habit I had picked up back in my teenage days. I had never read in the Bible where it was a sin, but I suppose I knew it was because after I got saved I always felt so bad about it. Even after I repented I still felt awful. I always made a promise when it was over I would not do it again, but no matter how hard I tried I could never keep those promises. There was always a next time.

Finally in the face of my despair my hope started fading. I knew that if something didn't happen for me real soon I was going to backslide. I was only hanging by a thin thread anyway. I had met this young man at the employment office who thought I was cute. I thought he was kind of cute too, and I knew that if *something* didn't change it would only be a matter of time before I got with him. I rationalized with myself about being lonely and trapped. I had no money to go back to my husband so what else could I do? There was always this tug of war thing going on inside me. I didn't just give into it all. I battled some, but I kept losing the fight and sinking into a greater despair. Nights were the hardest for me and I dreaded them. At night I would be as frantic as a cat on a hot tin roof. I had no peace and I cried all of the time. Then one day, just when I was at the point where I could stand it no longer, my mother called to say she needed me to come home. She was having a major operation and she wanted me there. My birthday was coming and she was sending me a ticket as a present so I could come home. Y-e-s! Thank you God! Of course I didn't even think about how wonderful it would be to see my family again. All I could think was "Baby your good thang is coming home to you and I'm going to rock your world." It felt like I had just received a pardon or something. I was finally going home to see my Honey.

Just to show you how naïve I was in my thinking, I had not even speculated about what he was doing while I was away. I suppose I expected we would just pick up where we left off and continue on with our marriage as if nothing had occurred. You know, sometime it's hard to face the truth even when it's knocking you down and standing right on our chest. Do I need to tell you what I found when I got there? Yes. He had moved another woman into our apartment and they were sleeping in the bed that *my* Grandma bought for us. I was so hurt I don't know why I didn't just drop dead right there on the spot. There is this strange thing that happens to me when I face total overload. Until that day I had only experienced it one time before when my father passed away, but when things get to be way too much for me I just shut down. I feel at first like I am going to totally explode and then it just fizzles out to nothing and I shut down. Weird huh? This whole thing seemed bitter cold to me. I had never experienced anything so horrible in my entire twenty years of life. What was I to do now? Although I was asking myself that question I honestly had no idea where I would muster enough strength to do anything at all. I was very distraught yet very calm. In the midst of my now calm demeanor murder was rising up in my heart. No I didn't kill him. I probably came closer to murder at that moment than ever before in my life, but no I didn't kill him. Without a word I just grabbed my baby up, turned on my heels and went home to my Grandma. Let's just say God kept me.

My Life
Still Chained

Chapter Three
Freedom vs. Bondage

It took me quite a while to get back on my
feet after that ordeal. To be honest it actually
took me several years to get over him. Shortly
after that (get this) he moved to California.
That helped me a little, but I still had to deal
with my strong attachment to him. I know, you
would think that after he cheated on me and all
I would lose my affection for him right? Not a
chance. I still wanted him no matter what. I
had this crazy love for him although we were
not really in contact with one another. Just
before he left the city he came by my house,
and he had the nerve to bring his girlfriend with

him. You will never guess who this girlfriend was? It was his niece, his sister's daughter. This was not speculation. He openly admitted this to me and my grandmother. He seemed to have no shame about what he was doing. I don't know but apparently incest was accepted amongst his family, and he was not the only one. His brother was going with her sister the other niece. I am not making this up. He was flaunting his incest like nothing was wrong with it. Who knows how long that was in the making? Well after that I knew I had to get on top of this insanity that was having so much control over me. I went to the mirror and looked myself square in the eye and said, "Girl, the man just does not love you. If he did he wouldn't treat you the way he does, so get over it!" That little gesture may not have worked immediately, but I knew it was a step in the right direction. It was the first time I was able to face reality head on. As hard as it was to deal with myself, I did it, and it helped me to go forward.

Once I was back at home I found a new church and got involved again. My new church's foundation was based on prayer so we prayed constantly. This helped me begin to get spiritually stronger. I learned the importance of a consistent prayer-life. I immersed myself in the young adult activities in our church. I joined the choir and made many new friends. We went to church all of the time. I don't think there was one day out of the week where nothing was going on at Church and that kept me busy. I moved out of Grandma's house and got my own place around the corner from the church so I could stay close. Unfortunately it seemed like no matter how busy I kept myself, most times my flesh was busier. As much as I tried to be in control of it, it always got control over me. I wouldn't sleep with anyone because that would have been too openly wrong, but I was losing my battle with masturbation more frequently. I repented many times over and I told God I wouldn't do it again, but over and over again I kept being taken by it. I prayed for myself, and

I also asked for prayer at the altar. Of course I didn't tell anyone what I was going through because I was too ashamed, but still I could not stop. I couldn't tell you which was worse, my body or my mind. Both were working overtime against me and I became secretly despondent. I really wanted to live a holy life and except for my sexual problems I was doing okay. I felt like Paul must have felt in the conflict of his mind when he wrote. *Romans 7:15-24 "For that which I do I allow not: for what I would, that do I not; **but what I hate, that I do.** If then I do that which I would not, I consent unto the law that it is good. Now then it is no more I that do it, but sin that dwells in me. For I know that in me (that is, in my flesh,) dwells no good thing: **for to will is present with me; but how to perform that which is good I find not.** For the good that I would, I do not: but the evil which I would not, that I do. Now if I do that I would not, it is no more I that do it, but sin that dwells in me. **I find then a law, that, when I would do good, evil is present with me.** For*

I delight in the law of God after the inward man: But I see another law in my members, warring against the law of my mind, and bringing me into captivity to the law of sin which is in my members. O wretched man that I am! Who shall deliver me from the body of this death?" KJV

I was in a mad cycle of bondage and the enemy was tormenting me day and night. Finally when I could take it no longer thoughts of suicide began to enter my mind. One day I thought maybe I would turn the gas on and sleep my problems away. Only God could have kept me from following through with it because for me it appeared to be so simple. Just set it and forget it. I even tried it once, but I changed my mind before too long and cut it off. Then on another occasion as I was gazing out of my 6th floor window Satan said, "Why not just jump out of this window and end it all? You are so high up you will probably be unconscious by the time you hit the ground and you won't feel anything. Go ahead. Jump! JUMP!" The pressure was so great and the command so loud I grabbed my head and literally began screaming, 'GOD HELP ME!" It is at times like this you know God is real. Even through all of the screaming I could clearly hear his calm voice saying to me, **"Matthew Chapter Four, Read It."** In a frantic haste I grabbed my Bible and began flipping through the pages until I found it. My eyes were so full of water I could hardly see. I wiped away the tears and started reading. Matthew four is the story of Jesus being tempted in the wilderness and his triumph over the pressures of Satan. Slowly a calm peace began to wash over me. At that moment I knew God understood what I was going through, and I knew He was with me in the midst of it all. Just hearing God's voice brought me a certain peace by itself. Collecting myself I settled down. I read the scripture over and over again milking every drop of encouragement I could get from it. The more I read the more I felt the soothing comfort only God gives come over me. It was like a warm blanket on a cold night. I started thinking I was going to be alright. I was sure my problems were gone forever now. I wish I could tell you it all ended there, but it didn't. No, I wasn't even close to an end yet. A couple of years down the road the enemy of my soul laid in wait with another trap.

I started pulling myself together and things got better for me, although finding a good job seemed to be a bit of a challenge. Remember I got married at sixteen so I didn't finish High School which meant no diploma. Things were rapidly changing in the world. Our people were becoming aware of the need for a good education. More and more Afro-Americans were seeking better jobs as the factories began closing down and moving the plants out of the country. It was the seventies and great change was on the horizon. At that time it seemed the largest salary I could make was ninety dollars a week; seventy five after taxes. That was by no means enough to support me and my child, therefore I needed to get my diploma. I wasn't going to spend an eternity in night school either. I just didn't have the patience for that sort of thing so I took the GED test straight out. Guess what? I passed it with flying colors. Isn't that something? I must have been smarter than I knew.

Three years had passed by now and I was back at home with Grandma. I couldn't keep the rent up so I lost my apartment. It was okay. I didn't mind too much because we helped each other. She took care of my daughter for me, this way I could work, and I helped with the bills which made things real sweet. I had a new job now too. There were even times when I worked an extra side job to have extra money. Yeah things were starting to really look up.

Being back at home did a lot to help with my loneliness too. I was always surrounded by family. My aunt still lived there after her husband died, and so did my two cousins. Both of them were married and had children which made the house always full and noisy. My cousins had been raised around me so they were like my sisters. Like sisters we often argued and got into disagreements, nothing too serious though. I slept in my own little bedroom I had from childhood. It was really a little too small for us now, but I didn't complain because it gave me some much needed privacy. I didn't complain but my Grandma did. She wanted me to have the larger bedroom my aunt occupied. Eventually I was able to get in there. My cousins finally moved out and when my aunt went to the hospital for a minor surgery on her hand, Grandma moved her right out into one of the smaller rooms and gave the big one to me. I was so happy to finally stretch out. I bought new furniture and wallpaper. I made it real nice for me and my daughter. All during this time I was working and going to church. I finally had a decent life. It had been such a long haul for me just to get this far. I had friends at church that were like family. Although we had our individual trials and tribulations we were a kind of support group for one another. I was still married legally, but since we had no contact with each other I felt like I was single. I wasn't fooling myself any longer. I knew my marriage was over for good, and I didn't look for anything else to come out of it. I knew the church frowned on divorce. It was never an option for me anyway. Who had that kind of money; certainly not me? There were times however when I did ponder the thought of divorce with the hope maybe one day God would have an answer for me. I was still very young and I had my whole life ahead of me. No. I was much too young to consider a lifetime of singleness. I wanted to have a family with a home, a husband and children. I had truly hoped singleness wouldn't be my plight. Was God going to make me pay for the rest of my life for one mistake? These questions plagued my mind because at church they told me the scripture says no divorce, and anyone who married me if I got one would be an adulterer. How gosh awful harsh that seemed to me, I was only in my early twenties. Stuff like that can cause a girl to pray the kind of prayers that probably should not be prayed by anyone. Much to my shame I admit I prayed for God to kill him. I knew it was far out there but, I just needed a reprieve any way I could get one. You know of course God didn't kill him, but you do have to be careful what you pray for and speak about in the open. Satan is always listening.

Remember I told you the enemy had a trap set? Yes he did, and I fell right into it. Believe me Satan knows just how to set you up. He capitalizes on whatever weakness you may have. I wasn't in the lonely despair place anymore, but so many times I had just wished for a friend to have dinner with and to share conversation with. Although I still had urges they only seemed to be out of control when I was left alone and became lonely. I was at home with my family now so I wasn't being driven into this trap by that.

The sad part is that it was all right there in front of me, but I still didn't see it. This guy worked so hard to get me, and then he just used me for sex. Thank God I didn't really fall in love with him. I was scared to death to fall in love again. I had feelings for him but I worked hard to keep it real. The only reason he got my attention in the first place was because he appeared safe. He seemed so nice. He didn't go to church, but he didn't drink or party either. Safe or not I knew I had to watch that love stuff. When I would think of all the rejection and pain I went through in the past, it made me afraid out of my mind to love any man.

It was so very hot and heavy in the beginning. After all I had been celibate for at least six years. I never really meant for anything to happen, but every night when I came in he was waiting for me in front of my house. I had no idea where he came from. Somehow he already knew my name and he introduced himself to me with a certain confidence that should have set off an alarm. We would just talk to one another, and when he would reach out to me I would shyly push his hands away. He didn't give me any problems about it and I thought it was because he respected me. After all, he knew I was a church girl. Before long he was coming over to spend the evenings with me. I would prepare dinner for him and we would just eat and talk most of the time. I rather enjoyed his company. Then we began snuggling on the sofa while we watched our favorite shows. Grandma was right in the next room so I felt safe. When he would leave we would kiss. He would try every now and then to get a little feel but I would always push him away and he wouldn't protest. This went on for maybe a month or so.

One night after he left the Devil said to me, "you are not a child. You are a grown woman and you need to act like a woman." I thought to myself, you are right, I 'm not a child. Tomorrow night when he comes I am not going to resist him anymore. So, the next night when it was snuggle time he put his hand up my blouse. Before I knew what happened we had sex right there on the sofa with Grandma in the next room; doors open and all. It happened so fast it made my head spin as though I was in a drunken stupor. I thought we would just play around a bit, but no way. It was on and cracking.

After he left that night I was in great despair. I knew God would forgive me. He had forgiven me so many times before. However, I knew at that very instance I was going to do it again. I just knew it! It was all so crazy to me. I felt like I had just stepped into some weird episode of the Twilight Zone. I was intrigued by the prospect of more, yet despondent over having failed God. What a hodgepodge of emotions. None the less, the real breaking point came for me when one night I was in church and the Holy Spirit moved so mightily on me. I repented to God that night and made up my mind I was not going to continue on with this mess any longer. I left the Church feeling like a million bucks. When I got home I was pleased to find he wasn't waiting outside for me, but when I got in the house there he was in my bed. I'm serious! Remember how I told you about my family. This was not a new scene for them so they thought nothing of it. As he grabbed me and began kissing me I melted in his arms like ice on a hot stove, and all of my new found hope melted right along with me. In the midst of my insane passion I told God how sorry I was, and I confessed to Him I just didn't have strength up against such things. At that very moment I just surrendered. I couldn't fight anymore. Since I loved God so much I would not bring a reproach on Him with my behavior, so I left the Church.

Before a good year passed in the relationship he started to neglect me. He wouldn't call or show up. I would go to his house and he wouldn't be at home. It took me a minute, but when I saw myself heading down the path of pain and insanity again I knew I had to let him go. I was starting to revisit some of those old lonely feelings from my past. I was feeling abandoned again and the demons were trying to return. I was **not** going to have a repeat of that pain by any means. No not me. I was out of there without regret. It had almost happened to me again, but I came to my senses just in the nick of time. I made up my mind not to let myself fall in love with *any man* ever, ever again. I decided to just use them for whatever they were good for and forget the rest. I faced the reality I needed them for sex, but I needed to be the one in control from there forward.

When that was settled I really got loose. Not all at once, but I was snowballing. Before long there were many men in my life, even the man who molested me as a child. I hadn't seen him in quite a few years but just as always we could pick up right where we left off like no time had passed at all. Oh yes, he was back and this time we had a different relationship. Now I was older and better able to consent to whatever we did and we took it to the limit. Let's face it, this man was my mentor. He taught me every dirty little thing I knew. You have to know he was all too happy to reap the benefits of the perverted seeds he had sown into my life. We partied hearty. We had one crazy time after another until he started to become possessive with me. That was a definite no-no. Nobody ties this sister down, and nobody tells this sister what to do either. We would get into these heated arguments. It wasn't long before we had a major blow up and it was good-bye Johnny for real this time.

This was also around the time I began to experiment with drugs. I had long time discovered alcohol alone did much of nothing for me, so I began to add a little of this and a little of that to my "get high". I was cautious though because I never forgot about my parents. For sure I didn't want to fall into their trap so I tried to be careful (if that is at all possible). When I was high you could not tell me I was not God's gift to men. Heck any man would be lucky to have me. I was a real "hot mama", a regular "freak of the week" as they called it back then. I even played the "Playas". I actually remember one long tall good looking Papa I often fooled around with expressing his confusion to me. He wanted to understand how I could call him only when I wanted to lay up with him and never feel anything for him for real? That's just the game I told him. Why would I have feelings when we are just playing? Look, I just wanted what I wanted, and after I got it I was through until the next time. All I *needed* was to play with him. I mean, if I didn't play him he would have played me. That's the way I looked at it. Playing was all I was able do anyway, because I just didn't care anymore. I was only interested in doing what made me feel good. Satan was truly working his show with me. I knew I was hell bound so I didn't have a need to put on the brakes. It was full speed ahead for me. If I was headed for hell, then let it be on a band wagon. That was my philosophy.

Those were the kind of things my head thought about to justify the hidden unhappiness that was in my heart. I was going from one tired relationship (or sexual experience) to another. In my heart I really just wanted someone to care about me, but no matter how much sex I had, no one loved me the way I needed to be loved. Life for me was beginning to become extremely miserable again. I never knew why other women could have love but I couldn't. I always seemed to end up with some old tired somebody who had nothing to give me but sex. Maybe I really was what Grandma said I was. One day when I was about fourteen years old a neighbor called her and said she had seen me and a grown man coming out of a neighborhood hotel. Instead of her trying to find out who this man was that was taking advantage of her child, she went off on me. She told me I was nothing but a bed woman and no man would ever want me for anything else. She didn't even ask me what happened. I want you to know that assault on my character left me hurt and confused for many years. It also made me feel that I was responsible for making those things happen. I couldn't understand. Why was my life like that? It certainly seemed true. I mean after all, this was all I had known all of my life. I didn't choose to be this way, it chose me. Her statement sounded like a pronounced judgment over my life. "A bed woman"? How degrading! What was wrong with me?

By now I was almost thirty years old and I had begun to have some life shattering experiences. I had gotten pregnant by this young twenty three year old guy who I had sex with only one time. I was working as a barmaid on the weekends and I had met this young man at the bar. Although he talked to me a lot I never really put two and two together that he had any interest in me. Personally I thought he was after my best girlfriend who hung out with me all of the time. One night just before the bar closed my girlfriend needed to go home early and she told me he was going to see her to a cab. I didn't give it a thought because I knew the routine. I figured they would leave together and take care of their business together and that's how we did. So when he returned to the bar I was a little baffled, but I figured I would get the low down later. Usually when we left the bar we went to the after hours spot. That night was no different except Dude wanted to go there with me. After a while I got tired and wanted to go home so he decided he would get me a cab. When I got ready to get into the cab he grabbed me and kissed me. He left me totally in shock all the way home. Wow! It was now out in the open. He was after me not my best girl. I really didn't have feelings for him like that. Most of the time I just resisted, but one night I fell prey to him when I was just too tired to resist anymore. All night he had been pressing me to let him take me home. Finally in my exhaustion I gave in and let him take me home. When I got home I was really tired so he ran me a hot bath and the rest is history.

Shortly after that I met this older man who told me he was looking for a good woman to share his life with. No, he didn't mean marriage, just shacking. By then I was really getting tired of the street games and I felt I needed to slow down so I let this man into my life. I thought perhaps he was just what I needed, someone who was stable and didn't want to play. I thought it would give me a sense of security. I didn't have any real feelings for him. I just wanted security and I thought he would be the one to give it to me. He was real cool. He didn't try to change me or anything. He didn't even mind me running the street all the time. He worked at night as a cab driver so whenever I was out and needed to get to another club or party, all I had to do was call and he would come and take me where I wanted to go. That made him feel good too because most of the time I was with my girls and he knew that, so it didn't disturb our relationship. However, about two months into the relationship I found out I was three months pregnant. I knew it wasn't his baby because we hadn't been together long enough. I didn't play games with him. I told him the truth about the pregnancy without beating around the bush. At first he appeared to be cool with it. Then he had the nerve to tell me to get an abortion. I said WHAT? Was he crazy or something? Not one drop of his blood would be spilled so I guess that *was* an easy solution for him. I was making him a plate of food at the time. I don't know what came over me but I threw that plate of food all the way across the living room at him. I tell you peas and rice went flying everywhere. It was time for him to depart.

So now here I am pregnant. I don't know why but it never disturbed me that I was alone in this thing. Maybe it was because I didn't really want the baby's father in my life anyway. I had had a terrible time getting rid of him. He was such a leech. He would show up on my job uninvited. He was always in my way cramping my style, but since Grandma told me he had a right to know I contacted him and told him. He didn't even question me. Now Mr. Security guy is gone, and Leech Dude ends up back in my life. Hooray for me!

In the fourth month the doctor discovered I was carrying twins. I was happy about that although it was a very hard pregnancy for me. I felt so stuffed all of the time I was sure I would burst. Then in the third trimester when my body could take it no more, my water broke and I gave birth early. The twins' lungs were not fully developed and they only lived a few days. The labor had been hard and long; nearly thirty six hours. Then I had to go through their death. Their father was nowhere to be found in the midst of all this. I guess he was too much of a coward. They called him but he didn't come. Why would I be surprised?

The loss of my babies was extremely hard for me to take, and it left me feeling hurt and empty. This was one of those things that literally knocks you to your knees. In fact I was so hurt I didn't know what to do with myself. As it turned out I had so many complications with the delivery I had to stay in the hospital for several weeks. I cried so much they called a psychiatrist for me to talk to. He told me he would have been more concerned if I didn't experience this grief. He said it was normal for me to feel the way I did. That was good to know, but not much relief, so I called my Pastor. What a huge mistake that was. Do you know what he told me? He told me God was punishing me for backsliding. Well that was just great! Now even God had turned against me. My life was such a horrible mess. It was all too much pain for me, so I shut down and Mr. Weed and Mr.Valium became my best friends. In my heart I knew when I got ready to resume life I could, but for now I just needed to shut down.

After a while I started to recover and I needed to get a new perspective on things, so I decided to think on something that would make me happy. Before I got pregnant I had met this real cute guy. He and I had begun to be good friends so I decided I would get myself together and go after him. I bought some new clothes. That always makes a woman feel good. I got my hair cut into a cute style and I went for it. I got him too, and after five years of living together and three children, we got married. He had proposed to me when I was pregnant with the first child but you know how I felt about marriage. I just didn't trust it. I loved him though. I knew I did and secretly inside I felt if I married anybody at all it would probably be him. We appeared to be a match made in heaven. How much heaven really had to do with this one I am still not sure about till this day?

Lord, we had so much fun together. We would laugh and laugh. Even when we were apart from each other I would think of something funny he said and almost laugh out loud to myself. We had fun in bed too. He was just as perverted as I was which made it real good for a while, but I promise you no relationship can survive on sex alone. Sex is absolutely no substitute for real love. At first I thought I finally had it (real love that is). Sometimes it's hard to tell what something is like when you have never had it before. I was really scared to love him but he hung in there with me. When we found out I was pregnant he told me he wouldn't leave me, and he kept his word. I could sense he had a secret dark side about him though. Well as long as it didn't interfere with what we had, it wasn't important to me. Then something strange happened. When I got pregnant with my second child by him I lost my desire for sex. My libido just took a dive. It's hormonal and these things happen sometime. Even from the early months in the pregnancy I had trouble. I thought for sure he would understand it was only a temporary condition brought on by the pregnancy, but instead he turned on me. He became very angry with me. In fact he almost became vicious and he demanded I have sex with him. The whole thing was such a shock to me I sort of blanked out into a trance like state. To my recollection no man had ever treated me that way before. I had always had the freedom of choice in the matter. Even the man who molested me had not ever treated me that way. Looking back now I can pinpoint this as being the pivotal point of change in our entire relationship. From that day forward things were never ever the same between us again. It didn't matter what he did thereafter, I never again was able to believe he loved me. I still loved him so I stayed with him, but I was forever changed on that very day.

I gave him what he wanted even when it was uncomfortable for me. I just gave it to him like I was a dead person. I really felt like I was dead. Some part of Lunette died that day and there has never been a resurrection of her to this day. From then on if he didn't get it from me he would flip-out. If I resisted too much he would retaliate by getting dressed up and going out into the streets for what he wanted. Over the years he demanded and demanded. Then when nothing much was left of me he began to tell me how inadequate I was as a woman. He really didn't have to tell me that because I already felt that way. Our love making was one sided. I never wanted to touch him anymore. When we made love I couldn't face him. I always had my back turned. Before this I could hardly keep my hands off of him. I loved him, but somehow he had managed to kill all of the passion in me, and I honestly couldn't help myself. Can you believe that coming from me the "Hot Mama"? Alas, those famous words of my Grandma came back to haunt me again. "You are nothing but a bed woman and no man will ever want you for anything else."

I was now over forty years old and it was still there. It just did not go away. I had even come back to the Lord by then, but I still felt like her saying was true. Throughout my marriage my husband raped me again and again. Many times I just surrendered and gave in to him so I would have some peace. However, he was relentless. It was a shame I didn't get much out of the experience, but how could I when I had died way back in the beginning. I wish I knew what was wrong with me. Sometimes I tried real hard to find myself, but I just couldn't find myself anymore. There was nothing left of the woman he first met. Most of the time I cried after it was over because it always left me feeling so unloved and empty. My husband would always ask me what was wrong. I could never explain to him how I felt. I would pray and pray, but no matter how much I sought the Lord no answer came to me. When a need for sex would arise in me it was much easier for me to satisfy myself. I hated doing that, but I hated sex with him more. You know what? I think that I just plain hated sex. I mean look at all the pain it had caused me throughout the years. If it hadn't been for sex maybe I could have been a normal person. Actually I don't know if I really *hate* sex. Let me correct that. Maybe I just hate the fact that it always has to be such a ruling part of our relationships. Even if my husband took me out for dinner or movie he expected sex when we returned. Just having that hanging over my head was such a turn-off for me. It was as though I owed him something and had to pay him for being sweet to me.

I mean why can't anyone just love you without always having strings attached? Maybe it is because the women today are too accepting of the strings. They will do almost anything to get hooked up with a man, strings and all. It doesn't seem to matter to them what is involved just as long as they "*get that man*". He can be a lazy non-working good for nothing. Someone who is completely unworthy of them, and they come all unglued just because he said they were sexy. Don't you know sexy is no compliment? Neither is hot. That means a man is addressing your genitalia not your character, beauty, or your personality. He is telling you up front I want your body, and it could quite possibly leave "you the person" out of the picture. So when the fascination with you is over he moves right on to the next fascinating sexy body, because there never was any commitment "to you the person" in the first place. I was never like that after my first marriage. I could spot a game from far away. Of course I had my issues, but I was not willing to put myself in harm's way just to have a man. That's why when I hit the streets I didn't try to find love. I just used them for what I needed or could get. Not that it was right to do, or that you should do that, but I was not going to be messed around with anymore. You see, all I ever really wanted was to be loved. I just wanted someone to love me for who I am, but it never seemed to work that way for me. Plenty of men liked me and plenty of men were attracted to me. They actually thought I was a great person, but I am not *sure* any of them loved me for real. What they loved about me was the way I was with them in bed. As far as the attraction thing goes, I have since learned it is spirits that attract spirits. Yes they know each other. Women think it is because of their figure or their beauty when a lot of times it is not that at all. A man can just look at you and tell you are a freak because it is really a demonic spirit that is in control of his lustful mind. The same goes for the women. Many times these spirits are ruling our thoughts and controlling our behaviors when we don't even realize it. I can't see that it was any different with my second husband either. Oh yeah, he married me. After all when he met me I was some great sexual package. In the beginning it was always hot and heavy. Maybe he was "drifting on a memory" as the Eisley brothers used to sing. I don't know. Then of course we had three children together. I knew he loved his kids, but that didn't necessarily mean he loved me. I probably couldn't analyze things at the time the way I can now, because if we want something bad enough we can psych ourselves into believing things that aren't really true sometimes. I'm pretty sure I probably felt it when we made love though. Oh yeah, I felt it alright! Looking back on those tears tells me I felt it. I had a deep need to be loved and not just sexed. In his mind he probably felt the two went hand in hand. Perhaps they should, but in what order? Should there be love and then sex, or sex and then love? If there is love first and then sex, people can focus on loving each other and the sex can be a result of the love, but if we sex first, then love is the incidental. So if there is no more sex, there is no more love. This could be a good argument for celibacy before marriage. So many marriages are breaking up these days. It kind of makes you wonder what their foundations were built upon to begin with; love or sex?

That's exactly why I believe God's way is the best way to do things. He protects us from these kinds of mix ups if we follow Him. What most men want in a wife is not found in sexually driven relationships. He wants a woman he can respect and love. Of course he wants her to be attractive and appealing, but how can he really trust her if she is willing to jump into bed with him the minute they get together? A man is a born hunter. The longer you resist, the harder he pursues. That's just the nature of the hunter in him. When his game is finally captured he wears his victory proud.

As I write this book I am baring myself in hopes of provoking you to some real thoughts about where you are in your relationships. If the pain is ever to stop then we have to begin to think more responsibly and truthfully about what we are doing. I say the madness must stop! If you set yourself up to be victimized then you will become a victim. What do you really want out of your life?

My Deliverance
Free At Last

Chapter Four
"Enough is Enough!"

After close to twenty years of struggle and insanity with this man my marriage ended in a crash boom that fizzled out before the explosion could really erupt. What I mean is I had one of those moments again where I think I am going to explode, and then I just don't. In my frustration and anger I picked up a kitchen chair to smash him in the head, and just when I thought I would take him out, the anger just disappeared and that weird calm came over me.

It was over and I was okay with that. I had had enough! I wasn't happy about it but I was okay. My relationship with Jesus had really blossomed over the years so I was able to find peace in spite of the whole thing. The Lord let me know it ended because *He* said enough was enough. Once God speaks it justifies and clarifies everything in your soul. It was settled. Jesus was all that held my sanity together anyway. I had learned to totally submit myself to Him right in the thick of things. I had to do it. So much of my identity had been lost over the years, not just my passion. I found myself lost in Mr. Sampson's world. I was even living my life tied up in his fears. I began to see how much of myself I had allowed to be restrained by my husband's idea of life.

As I went deeper with God he began to teach me more about my identity. I learned to stop defining myself by what others thought of me. I began to see myself as God sees me. The Lord made it clear to me there was greatness inside of me; greatness He had placed in me before I was in my mother's womb. I am so glad God was in control of all of this. If I did not have a new found security about myself the breakup could have taken quite a different turn. You see, I had neglected to tell you that a couple of days before the wedding I found out my husband was using crack. I had no real understanding of the devastation drug addicts and their co-dependent families faced, so I married him. Besides, I was sure he could get help and it would all be over with. I asked my aunt if she thought I should go ahead with the wedding or not? Without explaining to me why, my aunt told me she wouldn't put herself in that position, but I reasoned with myself. We had three children together. What else could I do? What's more, I was back in Church now and I couldn't go any longer living common law with him, so I married him. Oh yeah, and I loved him.

Never the less it was over now and it was time for me to go on with my life. I learned your children follow your lead so you have to keep it together so they will be able to also. I knew how to play that role well. I had been playing it for many years just to keep things going. That is what I did on the outside. On the inside it was a whole different story. Inside I was afraid. I wasn't afraid of being alone as I had been in the past. In this marriage I had spent many days and nights alone while my husband chased after drugs. (He probably was chasing after women too). No. I was afraid of going through the same scenario as I had gone through with the breakup of my first marriage. I just couldn't allow myself to suffer the pain and anguish I had gone through before, so I went to God about it. I remember saying to him, Lord if this is the way you want it to be then that's fine with me, but please help me to not go through what I went through before. I am getting too old now. I don't want to suffer in my flesh. I don't want to be burning and longing for him. I don't want to spend my days pining away for him, hoping and praying you will save him and send him back to me like I did before. You know I was so in love with my first man. The Lord said to me."You were not in love, you were in need." I replied,

Yes I was Lord. Don't you remember? I loved that man so much it took me several years to get over him. The Lord repeated it to me again, "You were not in love, you were in need, and I will show you where the need was created in your life." Then just as though I was watching a movie screen He took me back to the bathroom where I had my first encounter with the man who molested me at the tender age of two or three. I had actually forgotten about that experience but I was reliving the whole thing right before my very eyes. God then began to explain things to me. He told me that the enemy was able to get in and attack my life because I did not have a father to cover and protect me. Fathers are there to protect as well as provide for their families. I said, "Okay Lord. I understand but I'm fine now. I have been one of the blessed ones. It has not really affected my life." God said, "Oh yes it has. When that man imposed himself on you he released sexual demon spirits in your life. Spirits are transferable and those sexual demon spirits have remained with you to oppress you all of these years. That's where the perversion in your life came from. This is where your addiction to masturbation got a hold of you. You were not just born a highly sexual person. No. Those spirits were passed on to you by the man who molested you. By the way God said, that man was a pedophile. Yes a pedophile! You have not come to terms with this yet but it was not your fault this happened. He was the responsible adult and no matter what your Grandmother said, he had no right to put his filthy hands on you. Since those spirits affected your self-image, they have influenced all of your choices and decisions throughout your life. They have especially influenced your relationship choices of men. That is why you have perpetually made the same mistakes over and over again. You could not see yourself as anything other than a sex object; therefore you could not present yourself as anything other than a sex object. You have relied on men (who did not even know who they were themselves) to validate you and make you feel good about yourself." All I could say was WOW! For the first time in my entire forty nine years my eyes were fully opened. Can you believe it? It was not my fault. I was assaulted and left with this ugly stigma on me all these years. This was most incredible!

I want you to understand this is not just some random story. These are tear stained pages of my life. As I wrote this book I relived the pain of every experience. Many of you have had the same type of experiences in your life. Perhaps just as it was with me you have buried them so deep you may have trouble remembering what happened. Sometimes we bury things so deep we can actually think they are gone, but they are not. You may even think, oh well, I can't do anything about it now, but I have written this story because **you must** do something about it.

Over the years I have had the privilege of being in leadership and in ministry. I have watched the women's behaviors. So many of you are hurting in deep places and you may even think your pain is covered up, but it is not. You can dress up the outside, but your pain still seeps out when you least expect it. Often your pain shows up in your super sensitivity. No one can say anything to you without you getting riled. You are like a bomb waiting to explode. Everything appears to be an attack on you, so you have attitudes and anger all of the time. You rationalize that it is okay because that's just the way you are. Not so. It is your pain showing.

Your pain shows in your insecurities and your low self- esteem. You want to feel good about yourself, but you just can't. In most cases wel either over compensate for it, or let ourselves go. Since we tend to dress as we feel, our clothing choices can speak volumes about us. Some of you dress so provocatively. Maybe the girls think it is a display of your confidence, but for a discerning eye there is no cover up. Your insecurities and pain are showing.

I see this all the time how so many women are either jealous or prideful. Jealousy and pride are two bi-products of the same root system of low self- esteem. Pride is a cover for low self- esteem and jealousy is an open display of it. These are all manifested behaviors screaming out SOMETHING IS WRONG! Your pain is showing and it's so big you honestly can't even cover it up.

Not all of your pain has come to you because of sexual addictions and problems alone. Some of this pain has come because of rejection. Somewhere along the line someone who you wanted to love you rejected you instead. I often wonder what can be more painful than rejection? It leaves an indelible pain in your heart only God can remove. Rejection is like a wrecking ball to our hearts, and the reason it's so damaging is God did not create us to be rejected. He created us to be accepted in the Beloved. (Jesus) The enemy devised this attack on mankind to destroy us. Whether it came from a mother who didn't love you, or a father who wasn't there for you, or a husband who cheated on you when he was supposed to love you, rejection brings the same type of destruction to whomever it comes in contact with.

When you are sick and go to the emergency room you are usually asked what your pain level is. So, on a scale of one to ten what is your pain level? I have to ask because if there is going to be healing for it we must first acknowledge it is there, and then confront it. Confrontation is an absolute must for this type of healing, and not all healing is instantaneous either; it's a process. Let me explain.

One day while we were relaxing my husband just came out of the blue and said to me"I am sorry for all the times I raped you." I was shocked because nearly twenty years had passed since those days and I had almost forgotten about it. While I never recovered totally from my loss of passion I did what I could to maintain some kind of sexual relationship with him. I still hated it and I still cried but I never withheld.

I wish I could tell you my answer was oh that's ok it's over and done with, but that is not even close to what happened. It was as though he opened up a fresh wound and I nearly went into a rage. I was so angry with him I couldn't speak. I know he was as surprised at my reaction as I was, but I couldn't help myself. The pain flooded me almost to the point of drowning me. I got up and left the room. I later asked God what was happening to me, and he let me know that was the healing process kicking in. There are stages to healing of any wound physical or emotional, and the process was beginning for me. I had to confront it first. I had to confront the anger, and then the pain, and finally the forgiveness started to take place.

The longer you try to avoid confronting your issues the longer it will take for you to get your healing.

Some wounds go so deep the healing stages are done in layers. I'll explain again what I mean. While the initial part of my deliverance took place when God ministered to me about how I got the way I was, it was only the beginning. It played an important part no doubt, but still it was just the beginning. The complete healing took several years. There was still so much to understand.

Shorty after God revealed things to me I took a ministry trip to New York City. While there I went to visit my aunt and uncle who lived in Queens. We were all just sitting around talking over old times. I don't remember why this came up but someone asked if anyone had seen or heard from John? He of course was the man who caused this entire sexual trauma in my life. Out of nowhere, without any thought what so ever, my mouth blurted out "That man molested me!" A hush fell over the room. Can you imagine the looks on their faces? It was as though someone had stolen their tongues. No one said anything at all. I didn't plan any of this, but it was out now and I felt so free. I had never told anyone in my family about any of this before, but now it was o-u-t.

After that incident I thought for sure I was through with all that mess forever, but there were yet more layers that still had to come off. This whole experience with my husband had changed me so much there were still questions in my mind. Why did I lose my passion? God revealed it to me over the years. He made me understand that when my husband forced himself on me, it was as though I was being molested all over again. It also destroyed the feeling of safety a woman gets from her man. A man should protect his woman, but instead I always felt violated and in need of protection. This was all in the subconscious. A matter of what was buried on the inside of my mind controlling my outward reactions, and there was still more.

Ten years or so down the line, after I had moved to Las Vegas and began to Pastor a church there. One Friday night while in prayer God began to speak to my heart concerning my now ex-husband. God began to tell me I needed to go to him and apologize for all I had put him through. What? Apologize? All of this time I felt that *he* was the one who owed *me* an apology for all the pain he put me through. You see, sometimes women can be so selfish. We always think about our pain experience, without ever considering the pain we have caused others. I personally had never once contemplated any remote thought of having caused him any pain. All I could see was me and my affliction. When God explained it to me, I was able to understand I had caused him a great deal of pain also in those early years. Of course I didn't mean to hurt him, but that doesn't discard the fact I had fractured his manhood. He was still very young when we got together (eight years younger than me) and I expected him to understand and tolerate it all.

I now found myself in a position where I needed to deal with this on another level. It was time for me to take responsibility for *my* actions. Repentance to God should be first, but healing comes to both when we repent to the person we have hurt. Remember what I told you about rejection. It literally wrecks a person's life. The Lord told me I had caused his unfaithfulness when I rejected him. He told me that there were times when he went out because he had to prove to himself he was still a desirable man. Now I understood for real why I had to go to him and apologize. He needed healing just as much as I did. God is a fair God who loves us all unconditionally. Being a Christian means we have to get it right across the board. I called him and let him know we needed to talk face to face. He consented to meet with me and when we were done he thanked me and actually gave me a big hug. He told me I really have a message that will heal men. Imagine that.

The Conclusion
The Doorway to Change

Chapter Five

Let the Healing Begin

Each one of these events was steps to removing the layers of hurt this assault had caused in my life. Even the writing of this story has managed to remove a layer of the shame that has plagued me since childhood. Although I never thought I would share with anyone the story of my sexual issues, here it is. Once we uncover the hidden, and put it into the open, it no longer has the same degree of power over us.

There is no doubt a process for you from which God will bring healing to your life. If you allow pain and fear to keep you from coming to that place, chances are you will never get there. Past experiences tend to shape our lives whether it be for the good or for the bad. Bad ones stunt our growth emotionally and spiritually though. Unforgiveness alone will keep you from moving forward and growing up. The Lord wants you to be whole and well. It is His will for you to prosper and be in health mentally, spiritually, emotionally and physically. I John 3:2 His prosperity is the kind money can't buy.

Some of you have never had real happiness. Just because you've come to accept the idea of not having it does not mean you have to remain that way. I wish I could tell you how many times I have scanned over my life and thought how different I would have turned out if it had not been for the Lord on my side. I tell you there is no substitute for His love, His peace, and His faithfulness.

I don't know where you are spiritually, but if you have not surrendered to the Lord and allowed Him to become your personal savior, you are cheating yourself. God has a purpose and a destiny for your life. You are not just here to occupy space. You are important to this world and you matter so much. Perhaps you would like to take a moment here to just stop and pray and ask Jesus to come into your life for real. Let Him know you don't want to run things anymore. Confess you have made a mess of things and you need his love and healing for all of your hurts. Pray for him to shake the spirit of confusion and low self-worth from your life. Ask Him to cause you to see yourself the way He does. Remember He is not angry with you. You have made mistakes but we all have. The bible says all have sinned and come short of the Glory of God, but there is no need to continue on in this way. Today can be the day of your new birth and your new perspective on life. Today can be the day you free yourself of all your bondages and past hurts. Come on. Open your heart to Him. The benefits of serving Him far outweigh all the thorns and briars that litter your life right now. Stop running and enter into His rest. Let Him heal you so you don't have to be a silent sufferer any longer. This is my story.

"Now from heart to heart and breast to breast we flow from Woman to Woman"

Love You

Apostle Lunette Sampson

The righteous cry and the Lord hears and delivers them out of all their troubles. The Lord is nigh unto them that are of a broken heart; and saves such as be of a contrite spirit. Many are the afflictions of the righteous: but the Lord delivers him out of them all. He keeps all his bones: not one of them is broken…….

Psalms 34:17-20 KJV